GREAT WHITE SHARK FILES

by Noah Leatherland

Minneapolis, Minnesota

Credits
All images are courtesy of Shutterstock.com, unless otherwise specified. With thanks to Getty Images, Thinkstock Photo, and iStockphoto. Cover - Maquiladora, nabil refaat, schab, A.Aruno, Jsegalexplore, KittyVector. 4-5 - Willyam Bradberry, Konstantin39. 6-7 - Sergey Uryadnikov, Enessa Varnaeva. 8-14 - Alessandro De Maddalena. 11 - BW Folsom. 15 - Dominique de La Croix. 16-17 - SciePro, Konstantin39. 18-19 - Andreas Wolochow, Jsegalexplore. 20-21 - Ramon Carretero, Sergey Uryadnikov. 22-23 - Shiva N hegde, SusanBrand.

Bearport Publishing Company Product Development Team
President: Jen Jenson; Director of Product Development: Spencer Brinker; Managing Editor: Allison Juda; Associate Editor: Naomi Reich; Associate Editor: Tiana Tran; Art Director: Colin O'Dea; Designer: Kim Jones; Designer: Kayla Eggert; Product Development Assistant: Owen Hamlin

Library of Congress Cataloging-in-Publication Data is available at www.loc.gov or upon request from the publisher.

ISBN: 979-8-89232-061-0 (hardcover)
ISBN: 979-8-89232-535-6 (paperback)
ISBN: 979-8-89232-194-5 (ebook)

© 2025 BookLife Publishing
This edition is published by arrangement with BookLife Publishing.

North American adaptations © 2025 Bearport Publishing Company. All rights reserved. No part of this publication may be reproduced in whole or in part, stored in any retrieval system, or transmitted in any form or by any means, electronic, mechanical, photocopying, recording, or otherwise, without written permission from the publisher. Bearport Publishing is a division of Chrysalis Education Group.

For more information, write to Bearport Publishing, 5357 Penn Avenue South, Minneapolis, MN 55419.

CONTENTS

The Great White Shark 4
Diet............................6
Mouth 8
Nose..........................10
Eyes 12
Skin...........................14
Skeleton 16
Fins 18
Tail 20
Life Cycle 22
Glossary 24
Index 24

THE GREAT WHITE SHARK

There are many kinds of fish in the ocean. But few are as deadly as the great white shark!

Great white sharks are much larger than many other fish. They can grow to be more than 20 feet (6 m) long.

DIET

Great white sharks are apex **predators** of the ocean. This means they are the top hunters in their **environment**.

These sharks eat many different animals. They hunt other fish, dolphins, seals, birds, and more.

A SEAL

MOUTH

A great white shark is known for its big mouth! It has about 300 sharp teeth that sit in 7 different rows.

When a tooth falls out, another one moves forward to take its place. A great white grows and loses thousands of teeth during its life.

NOSE

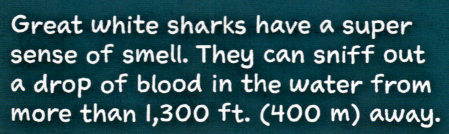

Great white sharks have a super sense of smell. They can sniff out a drop of blood in the water from more than 1,300 ft. (400 m) away.

AMPULLAE

They also find **prey** another way. Great whites have many small holes in the skin on their faces. These are called ampullae (AM-pull-ee). They help the predators sense things in the water.

11

EYES

The eyes of great white sharks look black. However, they are actually a very dark blue.

EYE ROLLED BACK

Great whites can roll their eyes back in their heads. This **protects** their eyes when they bite into something.

SKIN

Great whites are covered in small toothlike **scales**. The scales make their skin feel very rough.

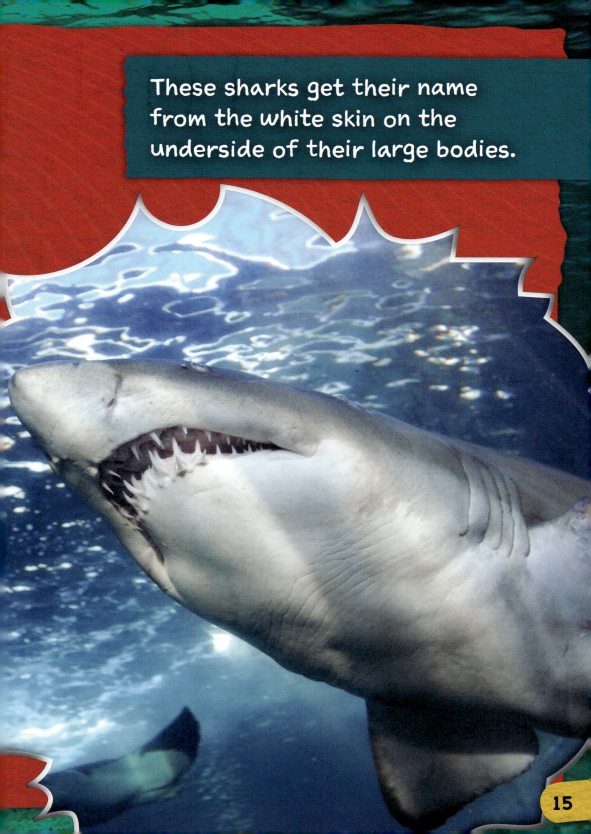

These sharks get their name from the white skin on the underside of their large bodies.

SKELETON

Sharks do not have bones. Their skeletons are made of **cartilage**. Cartilage is softer and more bendy than bone.

Cartilage is lighter than bone, too. This makes it easier for sharks to swim and float.

FINS

A great white has three main fins. The dorsal fin on its back keeps the shark from rolling over.

DORSAL FIN

Pectoral (PEK-tur-uhl) fins stick out from the sides of its body. They help the shark turn and stop.

PECTORAL FINS

TAIL

Great white sharks have strong tails. They move their tails side to side when they swim. This pushes them forward.

These sharks can swim as fast as 35 miles per hour (55 kph).

LIFE CYCLE

Great white sharks **hatch** from eggs. But this happens inside the mother's body. Baby sharks are called pups.

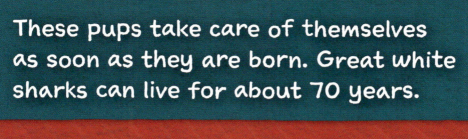

These pups take care of themselves as soon as they are born. Great white sharks can live for about 70 years.

GLOSSARY

cartilage the strong, rubbery stuff that makes up a shark's skeleton

environment the area where an animal lives

hatch to come out of an egg

predators animals that hunt and eat other animals

prey an animal that is hunted and eaten by another animal

protects keeps something safe from harm

scales small, hard pieces that form a shark's skin

INDEX

ampullae 11
blood 10
cartilage 16–17
eggs 22
fins 18–19
predators 6, 11
pups 22–23
scales 14
teeth 8–9